POST-IMPRESSIONISM

Jane Bingham

Heinemann Library
Chicago, Illinois

Produced for Heinemann Library by
White-Thomson Publishing Ltd
Bridgewater Business Centre
210 High Street, Lewes
East Sussex BN7 2NH, U.K.

Edited by Clare Collinson and Megan Cotugno
Designed by Mayer Media Ltd
Picture research by Amy Sparks and Clare Collinson
Originated by Chroma Graphics
Printed and bound in China by Leo Paper Products

13 12 11 10 09
10 9 8 7 6 5 4 3 2

Library of Congress Cataloging-in-Publication Data
Bingham, Jane.
    Post-Impressionism / Jane Bingham.
        p. cm. -- (Art on the wall)
    Includes bibliographical references and index.
    ISBN 978-1-4329-1369-4 (hc)
    1. Post-impressionism (Art)--France--Juvenile literature. 2. Painting, French--19th century--Juvenile literature. I. Title.

    ND547.5.P6B56 2008
    759.05'6--dc22

                        2008020464

Acknowledgments
The author and publisher are grateful to the following for permission to reproduce copyright material:
Alamy **p. 33** (Arcaid); Bridgeman Art Library **pp. 4** (Private Collection, Peter Willi), 6 (Private Collection), 9 (Art Institute of Chicago, IL), 10 (Musée de l'Annonciade, Saint-Tropez, France), 12 & title page (Burrell Collection, Glasgow, Scotland/ Glasgow City Council (Museums)), 13 (Pushkin Museum, Moscow, Russia), 15 (Wadsworth Atheneum, Hartford, Connecticut), 16 (Musée d'Orsay, Paris, France, Lauros/Giraudon), 18 (National Gallery, London, U.K.), 19 (Samuel Courtauld Trust, Courtauld Institute of Art Gallery), 21 (Museum of Modern Art, New York), 23 (Rudolph Staechelin Family Foundation, Basel, Switzerland), 24 (Musée d'Orsay, Paris, France, Giraudon), 27 (Private Collection/DACS), 29 (San Diego Museum of Art, Gift of the Baldwin M. Baldwin Foundation), 30 (Rijksmuseum Kroller-Muller, Otterlo, Netherlands, Giraudon), 31 (Rochdale Art Gallery, Lancashire, U.K.), 32 (Ashmolean Museum, University of Oxford, U.K.), 34 (The Barnes Foundation, Merion, Pennsylvania), 36 (Lefevre Fine Art Ltd., London), 39 (Private Collection, Christie's Images); Corbis **p. 14** (Burstein Collection).

Cover photograph: Paul Gauguin: *Nafea Faaipoipo: When Will You Marry?* (1892), reproduced with permission of Bridgeman Art Library (Rudolph Staechelin Family Foundation, Basel, Switzerland).

We would like to thank John Glaves-Smith for his invaluable help in the preparation of this book.

Every effort has been made to contact copyright holders of material reproduced in this book. Any omissions will be rectified in subsequent printings if notice is given to the Publishers.

Contents

Some words are printed in bold, **like this.** You can find out what they mean by looking in the glossary.

What is Post-Impressionism?

Take a look at the painting on page 5. It is by the French artist, Paul Gauguin, and it shows a group of **South Sea islanders** relaxing in the shade. Notice the picture's simple shapes and vivid colors. Look at Gauguin's use of different patterns and see how he has arranged his figures, with two girls facing away from us. Why do you think Gauguin has chosen to show the scene like this?

Gauguin was a leading Post-Impressionist artist. In his paintings, he showed his subjects from unusual viewpoints, and he used striking colors, patterns, and shapes. The result is a work that shows the world in a new way, through the artist's eyes.

Post-Impressionist artists all had their own individual styles and techniques, but they shared an interest in color, shape, and line. They avoided realistic colors and rejected the rules of **perspective**. Their aim was to create simple, striking pictures with a powerful emotional impact.

Who were the Post-Impressionists?

Artists known as Post-Impressionists include the famous painters Gauguin, Vincent van Gogh, and Paul Cézanne. Other well-known Post-Impressionists are Georges Seurat, who created a new method of painting, and the artist and poster designer, Henri de Toulouse-Lautrec.

The Post-Impressionist artists developed their new approach to art during the 1880s, and they continued to paint in their distinctive styles until around 1900. Most Post-Impressionist artists worked in France, but their styles influenced artists in other parts of Europe and in the United States.

Gaining a name

The Post-Impressionists did not gain their name until 1910, when the artist and **art critic** Roger Fry held an **exhibition** in London, England. The show included works by Cézanne, Gauguin, and Van Gogh. Fry struggled to find a title for the exhibition that expressed the different styles of the artists, but he finally settled on the term *Post-Impressionists*. This described the time when the artists worked—after the **Impressionists**. It also recognized the fact that they were all influenced by Impressionist art.

After the exhibition, Fry's term was soon used by other art critics. The name "Post-Impressionist" was a very useful way to describe the work of a group of artists who all responded in different ways to the Impressionist movement.

Taking it farther

Reading this book will give you lots of ideas for developing your own painting style. On pages 46–47, there are suggestions for how you can take your studies farther. These pages also include details of websites where you can view paintings by Post-Impressionist artists.

Try it yourself

This book takes a close look at the different styles and techniques of the Post-Impressionist painters. It also gives you the chance to try out some of their techniques. Look for the "Try it yourself" panels, and have a shot at creating your own images.

Paul Gauguin, *The Siesta* (1891–92). Like many Post-Impressionist works, this painting has a strong visual impact. Gauguin has used simple shapes and very bold colors.

Impressionism and After

Post-Impressionism had its roots in the Impressionist movement. Some Post-Impressionist artists started their careers as Impressionists, and others used techniques that had been first introduced by the Impressionists. Even though the Post-Impressionist artists rejected many elements of Impressionism, the Impressionist style still had a powerful impact on their approach to painting.

Impressionist rebels

By the 1880s, the Impressionists no longer seemed like rebels, but they had shocked the art world ten years before. While most artists in France were painting scenes from history, the Bible, or Greek and Roman mythology, the Impressionists had dared to be different. They had used an **innovative** new style to paint what they saw in the world around them.

Pierre-Auguste Renoir, *Summer Landscape* (1886). Critics of the Impressionists sometimes complained that their paintings lacked a clear point of focus, and said that their figures were not well defined.

Impressionist techniques

The Impressionists created paintings with bright colors and strong, bold brushstrokes that aimed to convey impressions of light, color, and movement. Instead of working in **studios**, they often worked outdoors, painting directly in front of a scene. They found new **subjects** for their art, showing landscapes and scenes of everyday life.

One of the most striking aspects of the Impressionists' art is their use of color. Artists such as Claude Monet and Pierre-Auguste Renoir liked to work with colors mixed from the three **primary colors** of red, blue, and yellow. They used a lot of white in their paintings and avoided black and brown as much as possible. The Impressionists also developed a new brushwork technique, applying many small dabs of paint.

Many of the Impressionists were strongly influenced by Japanese art (also see pages 14–15). They experimented with different viewpoints and created bold **compositions**, often framing their subjects in unusual ways.

Critical voices

By the late 1880s, some artists and critics had become dissatisfied with the Impressionist style. They thought that many Impressionist works were too vague and did not have enough visual impact. They also complained that the Impressionists simply showed what they saw, instead of planning their paintings so that they had a carefully

Who were the Impressionists?

The Impressionist movement began in France in the late 1860s and lasted until the beginning of the twentieth century. Many artists painted in the Impressionist style, but the most famous Impressionists were Monet, Renoir, Édouard Manet, Edgar Degas, Camille Pissarro, Alfred Sisley, and Berthe Morisot. Cézanne was an early member of the movement, but he is better known today as a Post-Impressionist.

balanced structure. Some artists felt it was time to leave Impressionism behind and take their art in some bold new directions.

Learning from the Impressionists

Like the Impressionists, Post-Impressionist artists used bright colors and strong, bold brushstrokes. They framed their subjects in unusual ways and concentrated on scenes from everyday life, as well as **landscape paintings**. However, Post-Impressionist artists developed their own highly individual styles. They used the innovations of the Impressionists as a starting point for their experiments in art.

One of the first artists to break away from the Impressionist style was Georges Seurat. Like many of the Impressionists, he was fascinated by the science of **optics**, and he experimented with creating different visual effects. However, Seurat took his experiments much farther than the Impressionists. He developed a new painting technique, which was adopted by several other artists.

Seurat's technique

Seurat created a technique that involved painting many thousands of tiny colored dots on his **canvases**. When his paintings are viewed from very close up, all that can be seen are clusters of dots of contrasting colors. But when the same picture is viewed from a distance, the dots combine to form a scene, with distinct areas of color. The technique of creating images from thousands of dots (or points) of paint is often known as **pointillism**. However, Seurat preferred to call his technique "divisionism."

Optical mixing

Seurat's paintings rely on a visual effect that was first explored by the Impressionists. In the 1870s, Monet and Renoir made an exciting discovery. They found that if they painted small brushstrokes of contrasting colors close together, the brushstrokes created an interesting effect when they were seen from a distance. As the viewer stepped back from the surface of the painting, the colors appeared to mix together to form a different shade. This effect is known as **optical mixing**. It is a way of creating very intense color effects.

Monet and Renoir achieved the effect of optical mixing by painting fine strokes of contrasting paint that look a little like short straws. In his early works, Seurat also tried this method, and in his first large-scale work, *The Bathers at Asnières* (1883–84), he used a "chopped straw" painting technique.

Pointillism develops

By 1885, Seurat had established his pointillist technique, replacing his short strokes of paint with tiny dots. Seurat applied his pointillist method to a series of small landscapes, but also to some larger scenes with figures.

Planning paintings

Seurat planned his paintings very carefully. Each element in a picture was deliberately placed to create a balanced, but unified, composition. Looking at *La Grande Jatte*, the viewer has the impression of a giant chessboard, with each of the 48 figures (and 8 dogs) carefully placed in relation to each other.

La Grande Jatte

One of Seurat's most famous pointillist works is *Sunday Afternoon on the Island of La Grande Jatte*, which was painted between 1884 and 1886. This large canvas is filled with figures of men, women, children, and dogs, strolling and playing beside the river. Like many Impressionist paintings, *La Grande Jatte* shows working people enjoying their leisure time, but it looks very different from a typical Impressionist scene. With its precisely drawn figures and its careful arrangement of different shapes, it illustrates Seurat's interest in **forms** as well as colors. Unlike most Impressionist works, the picture was painted in a studio rather than outdoors.

Georges Seurat, *Sunday Afternoon on the Island of La Grande Jatte* (1884–86). Seurat kept returning to this painting, and the final version was completed two years after he first started work on it.

Seurat's followers

During the 1880s, Seurat attracted several followers, who produced paintings using his methods. His closest follower was a young French artist named Paul Signac. Signac wrote a book explaining the ideas behind pointillist painting.

Lucien Pissarro, the son of the leading Impressionist Camille Pissarro, was one of the first artists to adopt the pointillist style, and he encouraged his father to try Seurat's methods. In 1886, Camille Pissarro created his first true pointillist landscape: *View from my Window, Éragny*. However, Camille Pissarro soon became frustrated by the limitations of pointillism. He believed that the style prevented him from painting in a fresh and spontaneous way. Within a couple of years, he had begun to introduce livelier brushstrokes into his paintings again.

Henri-Edmond Cross, *La Plage de Saint-Clair* (1906–07). Cross was one of the last artists to paint in the pointillist style. He specialized in very colorful, sunlit landscapes.

The "new Impressionists"

In 1887, the art critic Félix Fénéon gave the pointillist painters a new name. He called the artists the **Neo-Impressionists**. *Neo* means "new," and Fénéon believed that these painters would take the Impressionist style in an exciting new direction. However, Neo-Impressionism did not last long. In 1891, Seurat died tragically young, at the age of 32, and most of his followers developed new styles of their own.

One of the last of the Neo-Impressionists was Henri-Edmond Cross, who adopted the style around 1890, while he was working with Signac in the south of France. Cross used the pointillist method to create some daring compositions, experimenting with very unusual colors and using large and obvious color dots.

Printing with dots

The method of creating a picture by using colored dots was not just used by the pointillist painters. It is also the way that printers create images. If you use a very strong magnifying glass to look at a printed page, you will see the individual colored dots that are used to build up the colors on the page.

Try it yourself

Paint a pointillist picture
You can create your own painting using the pointillist technique. First, draw and color a simple picture with clear shapes and strong colors. This is the design you will use. Then use a very fine brush to paint lots of tiny dots very close together. For each color area, paint your colored dots in a variety of different shades.

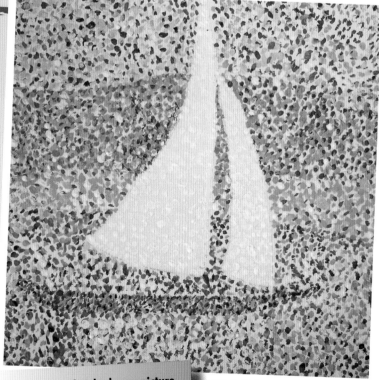

When you have finished your picture, stand back and admire the effect!

Cézanne's Style

As a young artist, Paul Cézanne was a member of the Impressionist movement. However, by the time he reached his forties, his art was moving in new directions. In the 1880s, Cézanne developed his Post-Impressionist style. His later pictures have a distinctive brushwork style and emphasize the solidity of his subjects. Cézanne's paintings often include clear horizontal and vertical lines, and many of his images are organized using geometric shapes, such as triangles or rectangles.

Paul Cézanne, *The Chateau de Medan* (ca. 1880). In this landscape, Cézanne emphasizes the vertical and horizontal lines in the scene. The result is a picture with a strong geometrical structure.

Paul Cézanne, *Still Life of Peaches and Pears* (1888–90). In many of his still lifes, Cézanne plays visual tricks. Here, he appears to have tipped up the surface of the table. This allows him to show the fruit and the jug from above and from the front at the same time.

A very individual style

In his later paintings, Cézanne developed a very individual brushwork technique. He used regular, diagonal brushstrokes to produce an effect that is sometimes used in pencil sketches. In many of his pictures, the brushstrokes change directions, creating a varied, patchwork effect. When Cézanne's paintings are viewed from a distance, his patches of diagonal brushstrokes convey an impression of depth and shadow.

Showing solid forms

Cézanne aimed to give a real sense of the solid, **three-dimensional** form of the subjects he painted. In the past, artists had achieved this aim by using the rules of perspective and careful shading. But Cézanne wanted to show solid forms in a new way.

In his **still lifes** of oranges and apples, Cézanne gives a sense of solidity by his skillful use of color and his varied brushstrokes. He also often shows the fruit from more than one viewpoint. Many of his paintings show apples and oranges from above at the same time as from the front. This technique has the effect of emphasizing the rounded, three-dimensional forms of the fruit.

Try it yourself

Diagonal strokes
Why not try copying Cézanne's method of using diagonal brushstrokes? First, look at the landscape painting on page 12 to see how Cézanne applied his paint. Then use patches of diagonal strokes to build up a picture of your own. You can use paint, felt-tip pens, or crayons to create your effects.

New Styles and Subjects

In 1886, the Impressionists held their eighth exhibition in Paris, France. This was to be their final show. Meanwhile, a group of adventurous young artists had gathered in Paris. They were inspired by the Impressionists, but they were also determined to develop their own styles.

The main figures in the new group of painters were Émile Bernard, Louis Anquetin, and Toulouse-Lautrec. Paul Gauguin was also associated with the young painters, and the Dutch artist Vincent van Gogh, who arrived in Paris in 1886, soon became a key member of the group.

The Petit Boulevard group

The group of artists that Van Gogh joined all worked outside the **mainstream** of art. He gave them the nickname "the artists of the petit boulevard" (*petit boulevard* means "small street" or "back street"). They often worked together or gathered in cafés to talk about art. They were excited by the Impressionists' bold brushwork and use of color, and impressed by the ideas of Seurat and Signac.

Art from Japan

Japanese art had an important influence on the Petit Boulevard group. By the 1880s, Japanese **woodblock prints** were on sale in Paris, and Van Gogh built up his own personal collection. He made careful copies of the prints and experimented with painting in a deliberately Japanese style.

Ando Hiroshige, *Night View, Saruwaka Street* (ca. 1857). Hiroshige's print uses very few colors, but explores the patterns created by the buildings and the people in the street.

In 1887, Van Gogh organized an exhibition of his Japanese prints in a local café, inviting all his fellow artists to come and learn from them.

A very different style

Japanese artists represented the world in a very different way from Western artists. Printmakers such as Hiroshige and Hokusai produced landscape scenes, often featuring people, but they did not try to show these scenes realistically. Instead, they created their own highly **stylized** view of the world. Japanese artists used large areas of **flat color** and clean-cut shapes. They often outlined their figures with strong black lines. They also framed their scenes in unusual ways, sometimes even cropping a figure so that only half of it could be seen. All of these elements of style had a major influence on the Petit Boulevard artists.

Louis Anquetin, *Street Scene, at Five in the Afternoon* (1887). With its limited colors and clear-cut outlines, this painting shows the influence of Japanese art. The scene is also very boldly framed, with a figure cut in half.

Japonism

Japan was completely cut off from the West until 1854, when the rulers of Japan signed a trading agreement with the United States. Other agreements followed, and within 10 years, many Japanese goods had reached the West. In Europe and the United States, there was a craze for the Japanese style, known as **Japonism**, as people rushed to buy fabrics and prints from Japan.

Paul Gauguin, *Breton Peasants* (1894). During his time in Brittany, Gauguin greatly simplified his style. He also began to use exaggerated colors. Gauguin's Breton pictures did not merely represent what he saw, they also reflected his personal response to a scene.

Gauguin and the Pont-Aven School

In 1886, Gauguin was 38 years old. He had been painting in the Impressionist style for many years, but he felt he needed to find a new direction in his art. He decided to spend a few months working in Pont-Aven on the northern coast of Brittany, in northwest France. Two years later, Gauguin returned to Brittany, staying from 1888 to 1889. During his two stays in the region, he developed a new painting style, producing works that were much simpler and bolder than his earlier paintings.

In 1888, several young artists came to work with Gauguin in Brittany. They all worked in a bold new style, using large areas of bright, flat color with strong, dark outlines. The group included Émile Bernard and Paul Sérusier. Later, this group became known as the Pont-Aven School.

Breton inspiration

By the late 1880s, Brittany was easy to reach by train from Paris, but the Breton people had a very different way of life from people in the city. Most people in Brittany still lived as they had done hundreds of years before, working in the fields and fishing. Most of the Breton people were deeply religious, and they held many services and festivals. On these occasions, women wore their striking traditional costumes—black dresses, with white aprons and collars and elaborate, white cotton bonnets.

The landscape of Brittany was wild and rugged. **Folk art** still flourished and the Breton churches were filled with medieval carving and stained glass. Gauguin found that the area provided many sources of inspiration for his art.

Gauguin's Breton paintings

Many of the paintings Gauguin created in Brittany feature peasants working in the fields, and he also shows women in traditional costumes attending church. While he was in Brittany, Gauguin also began to produce works with a religious theme. Two of his most famous religious paintings from this period are *The Yellow Christ* and *The Vision after the Sermon*.

In his Breton paintings, Gauguin moved away from using the rules of perspective. He began to see his compositions more as an arrangement of patterns and shapes. In many of his paintings, he experimented with unusual viewpoints. He also began to use very bold colors.

Try it yourself

Bold and simple
The Pont-Aven artists painted scenes that were brightly colored and very simplified. To achieve their effect, they used large areas of color with clear outlines. Why not create your own scene in this style? You can show a real view, or use a photograph or postcard as your starting point. Make sure you choose a scene with well-defined areas of color.

First, sketch your picture, reducing the scene to a bold design of colored shapes, with very definite outlines. Then use paint or felt-tip pens to fill in the shapes with vivid colors.

Use a limited number of exaggerated colours to paint the scene in your photograph or postcard. The effect should be bold, rather than realistic.

Van Gogh's Vision

In February 1888, Vincent van Gogh moved from Paris to the town of Arles in southern France. This was the start of a period of great creativity for him. For the next two years, until his early death in 1890, Van Gogh painted hundreds of pictures, in spite of several periods of severe mental illness.

Van Gogh in Arles

For his first few months in Arles, Van Gogh stayed in a hotel, but then he moved into the Yellow House. The house was a great inspiration to Van Gogh, and its simple rooms feature in some of his best-known paintings. In his studies of his home, Van Gogh manages to make a simple bed or a chair become filled with a sense of peace and contentment.

Vincent van Gogh, *Vincent's Chair* (1888). In this striking painting, Van Gogh uses color and brushstrokes to express the character of his chair.

Try it yourself

More than just a chair
In his studies of his table, bed, and chair, Van Gogh demonstrated that it is possible to create a very powerful picture of a very simple object. Why not try your own study of a chair? Try to use color and line in an individual way to give your chair a real "personality."

For the next year, Van Gogh stayed in Arles, and produced a remarkable selection of paintings. He painted many scenes of the local fields, river, and hills, as well as a series of portraits of himself and his neighbors.

Van Gogh painted entirely for himself, and he did not concern himself with selling his work. It is believed that he only sold one painting in his lifetime. In order to keep on painting, he relied on his brother Theo to support him (see panel on page 20).

Gauguin in Arles

In October 1888, Gauguin joined Van Gogh in the Yellow House, and for the next two months, the two artists worked side by side. They shared a love of bold, strong shapes and a vivid use of color, but they had very different approaches to painting. Van Gogh was a passionate artist, who expressed his emotions through his art. In contrast, Gauguin's painting was less emotional and more carefully controlled. Van Gogh liked to paint directly in front of his subject. However, Gauguin encouraged him to paint scenes from memory in order to create compositions that were more deliberately planned.

Vincent van Gogh, *Self-Portrait with Bandaged Ear* (1889). This picture was painted soon after Van Gogh cut off his own ear. The short, agitated brushstrokes convey a sense of the artist's troubled state of mind.

The two artists argued passionately about art. In the end, their quarrels became so intense that Van Gogh chased Gauguin with a razor. Gauguin escaped unhurt, but Van Gogh cut off part of his own ear. Gauguin left Arles hastily and the two artists never saw each other again.

Van Gogh in St. Rémy

In May 1889, Van Gogh entered a mental hospital in the village of St. Rémy, near Arles. He had been suffering from periods of severe mental illness and he needed a place where he felt safe. He stayed in St. Rémy for 12 months, mainly painting the view from the hospital windows.

Van Gogh's most famous painting from his time in St. Rémy is the moonlit landscape, *The Starry Night*. The painting shows a town under an enormous star-filled sky, each star surrounded by haloes of light. Like several of the works painted at St. Rémy, it features strong swirls and spirals, and conveys a haunting sense of anxiety and unease.

Last works

After a year at St. Rémy, Van Gogh moved to Auvers, near Paris, where he could be closer to his brother Theo. There he was cared for by Dr. Gachet, who he painted several times. However, while Van Gogh was staying in Auvers, his depression deepened and in July 1890, he shot himself.

In the last few weeks of his life, Van Gogh painted some large-scale landscapes. One of these scenes shows crows flying low over a wheat field, against a deep blue sky. With its jagged brushstrokes and dark, threatening colors, *Crows Over the Wheatfield* has been interpreted as a reflection of the artist's despairing mood.

Color and brushwork

Van Gogh used color and brushwork to express his emotions. His choice of colors was very significant and he associated certain colors with different moods. He used dark blue and black to express feelings of dread and fear, and lighter, brighter tones, such as turquoise and yellow, to create a sense of peace and calm.

Yellow was Van Gogh's favorite color, and he strongly associated this color with happiness and warmth. His paintings of sunflowers feature many shades of yellow in the flowers, their vase, and the wall behind them. The sunflower pictures were painted at one of the most hopeful times in Van Gogh's life, when he was preparing to welcome Gauguin to Arles, and they were hung in Gauguin's bedroom in the Yellow House.

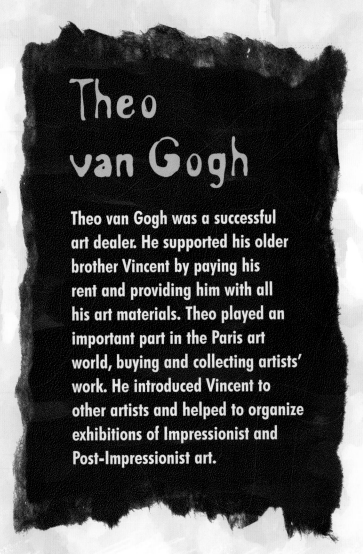

Theo van Gogh

Theo van Gogh was a successful art dealer. He supported his older brother Vincent by paying his rent and providing him with all his art materials. Theo played an important part in the Paris art world, buying and collecting artists' work. He introduced Vincent to other artists and helped to organize exhibitions of Impressionist and Post-Impressionist art.

Vincent's brushstrokes also reflect his mood. He used many short, broken strokes to create a sense of agitation, and longer brushstrokes to convey a feeling of greater calm. In many of his landscapes, the brushstrokes make swirling, circular shapes, creating a mood of restlessness and menace.

Unlike most of the painters of his time, van Gogh often used large quantities of paint, building up a surface that was covered with scores and ridges.

Vincent van Gogh, *The Starry Night* (1889). This painting shows the view from Van Gogh's hospital window at St. Rémy. Critics have seen it as a powerful expression of the artist's hopes and fears.

Gauguin in the South Seas

By the late 1880s, Paul Gauguin had grown tired of life in Europe. He admired the folk art of the South Pacific, and in 1891, he settled on the Pacific island of Tahiti. He spent most of the rest of his life in the South Pacific, and he died there in 1903 at the age of 54. Many of Gauguin's greatest paintings were painted while he was in the South Sea islands.

South Sea inspiration

The South Sea islands provided a great source of inspiration for Gauguin. He was amazed by the islands' natural beauty, with their brightly colored flowers, and exotic birds and creatures. The simple way of life and strong religious beliefs of the islanders made a deep impression on him. Above all, Gauguin was delighted by the physical beauty and grace of the South Sea people.

Gauguin was also influenced by the art of the South Pacific. He greatly admired the simple forms and strong lines of the native carvings, and he incorporated elements of their style into his work. His South Sea paintings are much simpler and more stylized than his early work. The pictures often include bold patterns, and some of his figures are deliberately out of proportion.

Images of island life

Gauguin's South Pacific paintings usually feature island people. The islanders are often shown relaxing in their homes, but there are also scenes of people eating, gathering food, and praying to their gods. The pictures are mainly painted in deep, rich colors, with startling patches of vivid color standing out against the darker shapes.

One of Gauguin's most famous South Sea paintings is the large panel, *Where Do We Come From? What Are We? Where Are We Going To?* It includes three different scenes, which appear to show different stages in the journey of life, from birth to death. Like most of Gauguin's South Sea images, the painting contains hints of sadness and fear.

Art of the South Pacific

The South Sea islanders have an ancient tradition of woodcarving. Carvers create powerful masks and figures, with unusual proportions and exaggerated features. They also carve decorations for their temples and homes, using simple, stylized designs, often based on island plants and creatures.

Paul Gauguin, *Nafea Faaipoipo: When Will You Marry?* (1892). This painting shows a young, unmarried girl with an older, married woman. On one level, it is a simple portrait of two Tahitian women, but it also has a deeper meaning, since the hopeful innocence of the young girl is deliberately contrasted with the sadness of the older woman.

Gauguin's symbols

Gauguin's paintings often include mysterious **symbols**. In *Where Do We Come From?*, Gauguin paints a white bird, his favorite symbol for death and the afterlife. He also represents himself as a leaping dog at the edge of the picture.

Artists as Prophets

In the summer of 1888, the young art student, Paul Sérusier, worked with Gauguin in Brittany. It was an exciting time for Sérusier, and he later came up with an ambitious plan. He would form a brotherhood of artists, who would create a new art for the future. The group was given the name "the **Nabis**," which means "prophets" in Hebrew.

Sérusier's experiment

In the late summer of 1888, Sérusier painted a picture with Gauguin's help. The painting, called *The Talisman*, showed a sunken stream in a clearing in the woods, but it was no ordinary landscape painting. In this important picture, Gauguin urged Sérusier to simplify his painting style, so that he concentrated only on shapes, patterns, and colors.

Paul Sérusier, *The Talisman*, or *The Swallow-hole in the Bois d'Amour, Pont-Aven* (1890). This painting was very important for the Nabi group. It is usually seen as the first Nabi painting.

Gauguin encouraged Sérusier to approach the painting of *The Talisman* in a new way. He suggested that Sérusier should not show exactly what he saw. Instead, he should use the colors in his painting to express his feelings about the scene. The result is a semi-**abstract** pattern that still gives the impression of the woodland scene he was painting. *The Talisman* was the starting point for Sérusier's new ideas about art.

Forming the Nabis

When Sérusier returned to Paris in the fall of 1888, he urged his young artist friends to paint pictures with simple colors and a strong personal meaning. By the spring of 1889, the Nabi group had formed. It included Maurice Denis, Pierre Bonnard, Édouard Vuillard, and Paul Ranson. Later, Félix Vallotton, a Swiss painter and printmaker, joined the group.

Nabi principles

Over the following year, Sérusier developed his ideas about art, and he established a set of **principles** for the Nabi painters to follow. Sérusier believed that artists should use very simplified forms. Their figures should have strong, confident outlines, and artists should aim to restrict their **palette**, using just three or four colors in a painting. Sérusier also urged the Nabi artists to turn to the work of the Japanese printmakers for inspiration. The Nabi artists rarely followed all of Sérusier's principles, but his guidelines helped them to create balanced and elegant compositions.

Some Nabi paintings featured pet animals. Perhaps you could show an animal in your three-color picture, as this teenage artist has done?

Three-color picture
When you restrict yourself to just three colors, you need to think hard about your picture's design. Try painting a picture with simple shapes and just three colors. Choose colors that contrast strongly with each other.

Nabi symbolism

Like the paintings of Gauguin, most works by the Nabis had a strong personal meaning, or **symbolism**. Symbolist paintings contain certain images or colors that have a special meaning for the artist.

Sometimes, the meaning of a Nabi painting's symbols is obvious to the viewer, but often the symbolism has to be explained. For example, Denis' painting, *The Cup of Tea or A Mystical Allegory,* shows two young women, one holding a tea tray loaded with cups and saucers. On one level, the painting is a simple everyday scene of two women at home. But Denis had very strong Christian beliefs, and he intended his painting to have a religious meaning. On a symbolic level, Denis' painting is supposed to show two priestesses offering a gift to the saint who protected their home.

A short-lived style

In 1891, the Nabi group held its first exhibition, featuring works by Bonnard, Denis, Ranson, Sérusier, and Vuillard. The exhibition was well received by most art critics, who appreciated the delicate charm and simplicity of the Nabis' work.

Despite the early success of the group, the Nabi painting style did not last long, and by the early 1900s, the members were developing different styles. However, the Nabi style continued to have an important influence in the **decorative arts** and **graphic design.**

Nabi designs

The Nabi artists believed in the power of art to transform people's lives. They wanted to bring art into many different areas of life.

Nabi artists worked in the theater, designing stage sets and costumes. They designed posters and books, as well as illustrations for music scores. They also created furniture, fabrics, wallpapers, and ceramics. Some Nabi artists designed stained-glass windows and painted large-scale **mural** decorations. The Nabi style, with its simplified shapes and limited colors, was ideally suited to interior and graphic design.

Art Nouveau

In the 1890s, there was a sudden surge of interest in the decorative arts in Europe and the United States. Many artists began to create exciting new designs for posters and books, and also for ceramics, furniture, and wallpaper. Around the year 1890, a new style developed in the decorative arts, known as Art Nouveau (or "new art").

Art Nouveau designs had flowing patterns and were often inspired by plants and flowers. Some of the Nabis' work was very similar in style to Art Nouveau, but their designs were usually simpler and less flowing.

Pierre Bonnard, *Le Grand-Lemps* (ca. 1892). This painting shows the countryside close to Bonnard's childhood country home. Like many pictures painted by the Nabis, it uses a limited number of colors and shows the influence of Japanese prints.

The Art of Toulouse-Lautrec

Henri de Toulouse-Lautrec was one of the artists of the Petit Boulevard, who worked together in Paris around 1886 (see pages 14–15). He was interested in the techniques of the Impressionists, but he wanted to develop his own individual style. He worked in a wide variety of artistic **media**, producing paintings, drawings, posters, prints, and sculptures.

Family background

Toulouse-Lautrec was the oldest son of a French count and countess. His family was very grand, but by the time he was born, they had lost most of their money. Henri suffered from many medical problems, which meant he did not grow properly. As an adult, he was only 5 feet, 1 inch (1.54 meters) tall. In his early twenties, Toulouse-Lautrec left his family home in the south of France and settled in Paris. He spent the rest of his life in the city, working as an artist and printmaker.

Many talents

Toulouse-Lautrec had many talents. He was extremely skillful at drawing, and he had the ability to convey a character with just a few lines. He also had a very strong sense of color and design, which he used to create striking posters.

In the 1890s, new developments in printing meant that posters were just beginning to be used. Musical theaters **commissioned** artists to create bold designs that would attract the attention of new customers. Toulouse-Lautrec was one of the first artists to design posters. He created powerful compositions, using a limited number of vivid colors, clear-cut shapes, and strong black outlines.

Life in Paris

Toulouse-Lautrec lived in Montmartre, a part of Paris known for its lively cafés, theaters, and bars. He recorded life in the area, especially at night, showing dancing girls performing on stage and also relaxing after work. Some of his works are finished paintings, but he also produced lively **pastel** sketches.

Try it yourself

Poster design
Posters need text to give information, but they also need a really bold image to make people stop and take a second look. Toulouse-Lautrec's posters were very effective because they had a simple, striking image. Why not try designing your own poster, to advertise a special event, such as a party, a play, or a rock concert? Keep your design simple and bold, and use just a few really strong colors. (Red, black, and white stand out well.)

Henri de Tolouse-Lautrec, *Poster for the Moulin Rouge* (1891). Toulouse-Lautrec's posters had an immediate visual impact. Here, he uses simple shapes, colors, and outlines to create a very dramatic scene.

Spreading Styles

By the 1890s, there were artists working in Post-Impressionist styles in many parts of Europe. The leading Post-Impressionist outside France was the Belgian pointillist painter, Théo van Rysselberghe. Meanwhile, artists in Germany, Italy, Switzerland, and Norway were influenced by the art of Gauguin and Van Gogh. In Britain, there was a flourishing group of artists who were strongly influenced by the Post-Impressionist approach, and the style also reached Canada and the United States.

Théo van Rysselberghe

Van Rysselberghe began his artistic career working in a realistic style, but in 1886, he visited Paris and saw Seurat's painting *La Grande Jatte* (see page 9). He was very excited by Seurat's new technique and he decided to rethink his whole approach to painting.

By 1887, Van Rysselberghe had mastered Seurat's technique and he continued to produce pointillist paintings for the next six years. He used the pointillist style to paint landscapes, portraits, and scenes with figures. He also encouraged other Belgian artists to work in the new style.

Théo van Rysselberghe, *Family in the Orchard* (1890). Some of Van Rysselberghe's best-known works show outdoor scenes, featuring women and girls in summer dresses.

Roger Fry, *Studland Bay* (1911). Like Cézanne, Fry planned his landscape paintings very carefully, using blocks of bold color and simplified shapes.

Roger Fry

The British artist and critic Roger Fry played a very important role in the history of Post-Impressionism. He organized exhibitions of work by Post-Impressionist artists, and wrote and lectured on key artists. He also produced his own Post-Impressionist paintings and encouraged other artists to turn to Post-Impressionist painters for their inspiration.

In 1910, Fry organized an exhibition in London that gave the Post-Impressionist artists their name. Two years later, he presented a second exhibition of Post-Impressionist works in London. In the United States, he worked with his contacts in the art world to promote the work of Cézanne, Seurat, Gauguin, and Van Gogh.

As a painter, Roger Fry was most deeply influenced by Cézanne. Like Cézanne's paintings, Fry's pictures are very carefully organized. Many of them show landscapes broken up into areas of bright color with strong black outlines, much like a stained-glass window.

Edvard Munch

The Norwegian painter, Edvard Munch, first visited Paris in 1885, at the age of 22. He was very impressed by the work of Van Gogh and Gauguin, and he began to create paintings with bold, flat colors and clearly outlined figures. Munch was also influenced by Gauguin's interest in symbolism. These elements all helped Munch to develop his very personal style, seen in paintings such as *The Scream*.

The Omega Workshops

Roger Fry was part of the Bloomsbury Group, a collection of **avant-garde** artists, writers, and thinkers. The artists in the group included Vanessa Bell and Duncan Grant. Bell and Grant were both influenced by Post-Impressionism. They created a variety of decorative arts, including poster designs, book jackets, fabrics, and ceramics.

In 1913, Roger Fry formed the Omega Workshops to make, promote, and sell decorative products that were influenced by Post-Impressionism. Fry, Bell, and Grant all produced designs for the workshop, and young "artist-decorators" were employed to work on the products and create their own designs.

The Omega Workshops produced a very wide range of items, including fabrics, carpets, painted furniture, lamps, trays, pottery, tiles, boxes, and jewelry. They offered an interior decorating service, painting murals and decorating furniture. The workshops lasted until 1919, and helped to bring Post-Impressionist designs to a wide audience.

Spencer Gore, *The Cinder Path* (1912). This painting was exhibited in Roger Fry's second Post-Impressionist exhibition, which was held in London in 1912.

Charleston Farmhouse was filled with the art of British Post-Impressionist artists. Now the house is open to the public.

The Camden Town group

The artists of the Bloomsbury group were not the only English painters to be influenced by Post-Impressionism. In 1911, a group of artists came together in the Camden Town area of London. The group included Walter Sickert, Spencer Gore, and Harold Gilman. Lucien Pissarro was also part of the group. He had moved from France to England in 1890, and helped to spread ideas about pointillism.

The Camden Town painters concentrated on domestic scenes and views of London and other landscapes. In the early 1900s, they were strongly influenced by the paintings of Bonnard and Vuillard. However, following Roger Fry's Post-Impressionist exhibition in 1910, the group began to use stronger colors.

The Camden Town group held three successful exhibitions, but after December 1912, they did not exhibit together again.

Charleston, an artists' home

In 1916, Vanessa Bell moved to Charleston, a farmhouse in the south of England. She shared the house with friends, including Duncan Grant, and Roger Fry was a frequent visitor. Bell and her artist friends turned the house into a work of art. As well as hanging pictures everywhere, she used Omega fabrics for curtains and chairs, and she painted walls, doors, and fireplaces with colorful scenes and patterns. Bell had a passion for decorating surfaces, and the house is full of painted chairs, chests, tables, and even beds. The result is a riot of color, patterns, and pictures—mainly inspired by the work of Post-Impressionist artists.

Maurice Prendergast, *Landscape with Rowboats* (1916–18). Prendergast worked in a Post-Impressionist style for most of his career. His paintings have been compared to tapestries and mosaics.

Post-Impressionism in the United States

Post-Impressionism had a powerful impact on art in the United States. Many U.S. artists had close connections with painters in France, and some began to work in Post-Impressionist styles as early as the 1890s. However, Post-Impressionism did not really take off in the United States until 1913. In that year, a groundbreaking exhibition of modern art was held in New York. Known as the Armory Show, it was intended to bring the American public up to date with developments in European modern art. The Armory Show included works by Seurat, Cézanne, Gauguin, and Van Gogh. The exhibition caused much excitement among artists, critics, and art collectors.

North American Post-Impressionists

One of the earliest North American painters to adopt a Post-Impressionist style was Canadian-born Maurice Prendergast. He spent some of his early career studying art in Paris, but worked mainly in Boston and New York. By the 1890s, Prendergast was producing lively paintings with exaggerated colors and flattened, patternlike forms. Prendergast often showed people in parks enjoying their free time, but he also painted a series of still lifes that were clearly influenced by Cézanne.

Young artists

Some young U.S. artists were clearly influenced by the Post-Impressionist works they saw in the Armory Show. In 1914, Stuart Davis started to use diagonal brushstrokes, in a similar way to Cézanne. Meanwhile, Georgia O'Keeffe created very colorful landscapes that resembled the work of Gauguin. Later, both these artists developed their own styles, but their early work shows the impact of the Post-Impressionists.

Exhibitions and dealers

Most of the Post-Impressionist artists struggled to sell their work, especially in the early years of their careers, and Van Gogh probably sold only one painting during his lifetime. However, there were places where artists painting in Post-Impressionist styles could show their work. Cézanne exhibited with the Impressionists, and the final Impressionist exhibition of 1886 was dominated by the pointillist paintings of Seurat and his followers. The annual exhibition of the Salon des Indépendants in Paris also became a major showcase for the work of the Post-Impressionist artists.

By the 1890s, collectors and dealers had begun to take an interest in the Post-Impressionist artists. The Paris-based dealers, Paul Durand-Ruel and Le Barc de Boutteville, concentrated on the work of the Nabi group and Toulouse-Lautrec, and the dealer Ambroise Vollard also promoted Cézanne, Gauguin, and Van Gogh. In 1901, the genius of Van Gogh was finally recognized in a one-man show in Paris.

Outside France, the work of the Post-Impressionists was regularly shown in Belgium. In London, Roger Fry held two major exhibitions of Post-Impressionist art in 1910 and 1912. Fry was also one of the organizers of the Armory Show in New York in 1913.

Making an Impact

The Post-Impressionist artists produced most of their work in the last 15 years of the nineteenth century, but their art had a powerful impact on the art of the following century. In the early years of the twentieth century, there was an explosion of different art styles, and many of these styles had their origins in Post-Impressionism. **Cubism, Fauvism,** and **Expressionism** all had their roots in Post-Impressionist styles.

Cubism

One of the major art movements of the twentieth century was Cubism. This is a style in which artists build up their paintings or sculptures using a collection of geometric shapes, such as triangles, cones, and cubes. Cubist artists often use more than one viewpoint, so their subjects are seen from several different sides at once.

Juan Gris, *Landscape and Houses at Ceret* (1913). Gris was a leading member of the Cubist movement. With its brilliant colors and bold outlines, his work is clearly influenced by Post-Impressionism. The geometric approach of the Cubists was also partly inspired by the landscapes of Cézanne.

The Cubist movement began around 1910, with the works of Pablo Picasso and Georges Braque. One of the major influences in the development of Cubism was the later work of Cézanne. In planning his paintings, Cézanne often used simple geometric forms, such as triangles and rectangles. He also experimented in his still life paintings with using several different viewpoints at once. This use of multiple viewpoints was explored by the Cubists in their paintings and sculptures.

Fauvism

The Fauvist movement flourished in the first ten years of the twentieth century. The word *Fauvism* comes from the French word *fauve*, which means "wild beast," and the Fauvists were known for their wild brushwork and daring use of color. The leading Fauvists were Henri Matisse and André Derain. In their paintings, they used simplified shapes and very surprising colors, showing flesh as green or trees as scarlet.

In their courageous use of color, the Fauvists were strongly influenced by the work of Van Gogh and Gauguin. They also responded to the strong, **expressive** brushstrokes in Van Gogh's paintings. Matisse was also influenced by the color experiments of Seurat and Signac, and he produced some early paintings in the pointillist style.

Return to Impressionism

While most artists of the early twentieth century were moving in new directions, two Post-Impressionist painters returned to the Impressionist style. In the 1890s, Pierre Bonnard and Édouard Vuillard were both part of the Nabi group. They produced paintings with strong outlines and they used a limited range of colors. However, in their later works, their style was much closer to that of the Impressionists. Their colors became more varied than in their earlier works and the outlines of their figures softened.

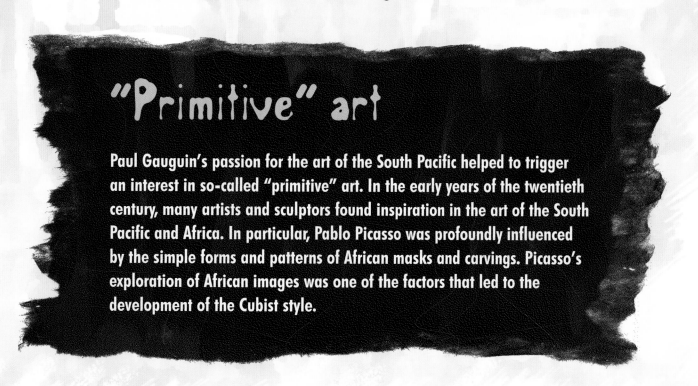

"Primitive" art

Paul Gauguin's passion for the art of the South Pacific helped to trigger an interest in so-called "primitive" art. In the early years of the twentieth century, many artists and sculptors found inspiration in the art of the South Pacific and Africa. In particular, Pablo Picasso was profoundly influenced by the simple forms and patterns of African masks and carvings. Picasso's exploration of African images was one of the factors that led to the development of the Cubist style.

Expressionism

The Expressionist movement began around 1905 in Germany, and leading early Expressionists included the young painters Emil Nolde and Ernst Ludwig Kirchner. The Expressionists were very impressed by the way the Post-Impressionists used color, brushwork, and shapes to express emotions. They were especially affected by the later work of Van Gogh, with its painfully expressive brushstrokes.

The Expressionists followed the lead of artists, such as Van Gogh, in their use of color and brushwork, but they allowed themselves even more freedom. They often showed very disturbing subjects, such as people suffering and in pain, and their painting style expressed the raw emotion of their subjects.

Emil Nolde was especially fascinated by the way that Van Gogh used different colors to express emotions. Like Van Gogh, he developed his own very personal use of color, with certain colors representing different emotions.

Symbolism

The Symbolist movement had its origins in the late 1880s, around the same time as Post-Impressionism. It included poets, musicians, and **philosophers**, as well as artists. Symbolist painters often used images from dreams, mythology, and religion to express what they believed was "the secret language of the soul." They included the French painters, Pierre Puvis de Chavannes and Odilon Redon, and the Norwegian artist Edvard Munch (see page 31).

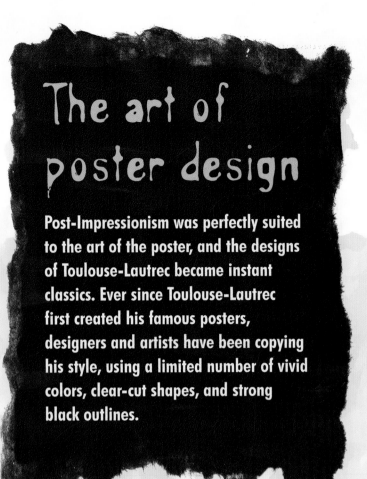

The art of poster design

Post-Impressionism was perfectly suited to the art of the poster, and the designs of Toulouse-Lautrec became instant classics. Ever since Toulouse-Lautrec first created his famous posters, designers and artists have been copying his style, using a limited number of vivid colors, clear-cut shapes, and strong black outlines.

The Symbolists were influenced by some members of the Nabi group, especially Maurice Denis. They also recognized the importance of the artistic style and ideas of Gauguin.

Optical experiments

The pointillist paintings of Georges Seurat and his followers marked the start of a series of artistic investigations into color and optics. In the 1960s, **Op Art** painters experimented with placing different colors next to each other to create some very surprising optical effects. Today, artists such as the British painter Bridget Riley are still experimenting with how we see color. Riley creates very striking abstract paintings, using stripes and lines in contrasting colors.

A lasting impact

Post-Impressionism had a lasting impact on the art world. The Post-Impressionist artists took Impressionism in new directions, forming a bridge between the Impressionists and the art of the twentieth century. Their interest in pattern, color, and symbolism inspired many later artists and designers. In particular, Post-Impressionism made an impact because of the vision of three great artists: Van Gogh, Gauguin, and Cézanne.

Ernst Ludwig Kirchner, *Sunflowers* (1909). Many artists have painted sunflowers as a deliberate act of respect for Van Gogh. In Kirchner's Expressionist work, the flowers are shown with exaggerated colors and painted with wildly expressive brushstrokes.

Lives of the Artists

Paul Cézanne (1839–1906)

Cézanne grew up in Aix-en-Provence, in the south of France. He moved to Paris in 1861, where he met a group of young artists who developed the Impressionist style. Cézanne painted with Camille Pissarro in the 1870s, but later reacted against Impressionism. In 1886, Cézanne settled in the south of France, where he concentrated on developing his own distinctive style. Cézanne mainly painted landscapes and still lifes, but he also produced portraits and imaginary scenes with figures. He came to be regarded as a leading figure in Post-Impressionism. Cézanne had a long artistic career and died at the age of 67.

Vincent van Gogh (1853–90)

Van Gogh was the son of a Dutch Protestant minister. He worked as an art dealer, a teacher, and a lay preacher before taking up painting full-time around 1880. For the next six years, he traveled in Belgium and the Netherlands. In 1886, he arrived in Paris, where he joined Bernard, Toulouse-Lautrec, and Anquetin in the Petit Boulevard group. He also met and worked with Camille and Lucien Pissarro, Gauguin, and Signac.

In 1888, Van Gogh moved to Arles in the south of France, where he was joined for two months by Gauguin. In 1889, following a period of mental illness, he spent a year in an asylum in St. Rémy. He then lived in Auvers near Paris, where he was supervised by Dr. Gachet, until his suicide at the age of 37. Van Gogh's mature art is remarkable for its expressive use of color and brushwork.

Paul Gauguin (1848–1903)

Gauguin was born in Paris, but he lived in Peru until he was seven years old. In 1865, he joined the merchant navy and traveled widely. From 1871 to 1883, he worked on the Paris stock exchange and painted as an amateur in the Impressionist style. During this period, he was taught by Camille Pissarro and he exhibited in the last five Impressionist exhibitions. In 1883, Gauguin left his job and became a professional artist. He traveled widely, working in Brittany, Martinique, Arles, and Tahiti. He died on the Marquesas Islands in the South Pacific, at 54 years old. In the late 1880s, Gauguin developed his mature style, which included strong decorative elements, a very individual use of color, and personal and religious symbols.

Paul Sérusier (1863?–1927)

Sérusier grew up in Paris and studied art at the Académie Julian art school. In 1888, he traveled to Brittany, where he worked closely with Gauguin, producing the revolutionary painting *The Talisman*. Sérusier went on to form a group of artists known as the Nabis. He visited Brittany regularly, eventually settling there. He continued to paint and produce decorative works for the rest of his career.

Paul Signac (1863–1935)

Signac came from a wealthy Parisian family. He was self-taught as an artist. He met Seurat in 1884, Camille and Lucien Pissarro in 1885, and Van Gogh in 1886. Signac was especially impressed by Seurat's ideas and by 1886, he was painting in the Neo-Impressionist (or pointillist) style. He also wrote widely about art, including some explanations of the theories behind pointillism. In 1892, Signac settled in St. Tropez in the south of France. His works are mainly landscapes, but he also produced some figure paintings. His later works moved away from strict Neo-Impressionism.

Georges Seurat (1859–91)

Seurat came from a wealthy Parisian family. In the late 1870s, he trained as an artist in the academic style at the School of Fine Arts in Paris. He did military service from 1879 to 1880. After returning to painting, he began to experiment with using color contrasts to create visual effects. In 1884–86, he created his first truly pointillist painting, *La Grande Jatte*. Seurat attracted several followers who adopted his pointillist approach, including Paul Signac, and Camille and Lucien Pissarro. In the 1880s, he continued to paint large scenes of modern life in the pointillist manner, and also produced smaller-scale landscape studies. He died at the age of 32.

Henri de Toulouse-Lautrec (1864–1901)

Toulouse-Lautrec came from an aristocratic family in southern France. Various medical problems meant that he did not grow properly. In 1882, he moved to Paris, where he studied with some leading artists of the day. However, he soon met Émile Bernard, Van Gogh, and Anquetin, forming the group known as the artists of the Petit Boulevard. In 1884, Toulouse-Lautrec moved to a studio in the Montmartre region of Paris, and from then on, he concentrated on painting life in the cafés and bars close to where he lived. He also produced posters, prints, and pastel sketches. He died at the age of 36.

1874 The first Impressionist exhibition is held in Paris, France. This is the first of eight Impressionist exhibitions held between 1874 and 1886.

1885 Seurat paints his first major pointillist painting; Pissarro meets Seurat and starts experimenting in the pointillist style

1886 Van Gogh arrives in Paris; the eighth Impressionist exhibition is dominated by pointillist works; the annual exhibition at the Salon des Indépendants in Paris includes works by Lucien Pissarro and Seurat (after this, some Post-Impressionist works feature almost every year in the exhibition); Van Rysselberghe visits Paris and sees Seurat's work; Gauguin stays for the first time at Pont-Aven in Brittany; Cézanne moves to Provence in the south of France, where he develops his ideas about painting

1887 Gauguin travels to Panama in Central America and Martinique in the Caribbean; Van Gogh organizes an exhibition of Japanese prints in Café Le Tambourin and an exhibition at Restaurant du Chalet, including works by himself, Anquetin, Bernard, and Toulouse-Lautrec

1888 Van Gogh moves to Arles, France; Gauguin and Bernard work together in Pont-Aven; Gauguin joins Van Gogh in Arles for two months; Sérusier works with Gauguin in Pont-Aven and produces his painting *The Talisman*; a group of Paris art students led by Sérusier form the Nabis; *Les Vingt*, a group of artists based in Belgium, invite Anquetin, Signac, and Toulouse-Lautrec to contribute to their annual exhibition, marking the start of regular showings of Post-Impressionist art in Belgium

1889 Gauguin works in Brittany; Sérusier joins Gauguin for the summer; Van Gogh voluntarily enters the asylum at St. Rémy; an exhibition at the Café Volpini in Paris includes works by Anquetin, Bernard, and Gauguin

1890 Van Gogh moves to Auvers, France, where he commits suicide; Lucien Pissarro moves to England

1891 Seurat dies; Gauguin goes to Tahiti in the South Pacific; the Nabis hold their first group exhibition, including works by Bonnard, Denis, Ranson, Sérusier, and Vuillard

1892 Signac moves to St. Tropez in the south of France; the second Nabi exhibition is held, including works by Bernard, Denis, Ranson, Sérusier, and Vuillard; a Neo-Impressionist exhibition is held in Paris including works by Cross,

Camille Pissarro, Seurat, Signac, and Van Rysselberghe; the Paris art dealer, Le Barc de Boutteville, holds an exhibition of Post-Impressionist works, marking the start of a series of 15 exhibitions organized by Le Barc de Boutteville between 1892 and 1897

1893 Gauguin returns from Tahiti to France; a Neo-Impressionist exhibition is held in Paris, including work by Cross, Lucien Pissarro, Signac, and Van Rysselberghe

1894 The first exhibition of *La Libre Esthétique* is held in Brussels, Belgium, featuring a major section on the decorative arts, and including works by the Post-Impressionists

1895 Gauguin returns to Tahiti; the Paris art dealer, Ambroise Vollard holds a one-man show of Cézanne's work; the first exhibition in the Salon Art Nouveau is held in Paris, featuring work by several Post-Impressionist artists

1896 Durand-Ruel, a Paris art dealer, holds a one-man show of Bonnard's work

1897 Vollard holds an exhibition in Paris, including work by Bonnard, Ranson, Sérusier, Vallotton, and Vuillard

1898 Gauguin attempts suicide after completing his painting *Where Do We Come From?*; the second one-man show of works by Cézanne is held in Paris

1901 Toulouse-Lautrec dies; a one-man show of works by Van Gogh is held in Paris

1903 Gauguin and Camille Pissarro die

1906 Cézanne dies

1910 Roger Fry organizes an exhibition in London entitled "Manet and the Post-Impressionists," marking the first time the term "Post-Impressionist" is used and including works by Cézanne, Denis, Gauguin, Van Gogh, Sérusier, Seurat, Signac, and Vallotton

1912 Roger Fry organizes a second exhibition of Post-Impressionist art in London, England

1913 The Armory Show in New York includes works by Bernard, Cézanne, Gauguin, Van Gogh, Seurat, Signac, and Toulouse-Lautrec; Roger Fry founds the Omega Workshops to create decorative arts in the Post-Impressionist style

Glossary

abstract showing an idea rather than a person or a thing

art critic professional person who gives their opinion, often in a written review, about a work of art

avant-garde very adventurous and ahead of the crowd

canvas strong, heavy woven piece of cloth used as a surface for oil paintings

commission pay in advance for a work of art to be created

composition arrangement of the different elements or subjects in a painting

Cubism early twentieth-century style of art based on geometric shapes. Leading Cubist artists were Pablo Picasso, Georges Braque, and Juan Gris.

decorative arts forms of art used to decorate rooms or buildings. Fabric design, mural painting, and stained glass are all types of decorative arts.

exhibition public art show

Expressionism style of art that aims to express the emotions, using very bold shapes and colors. Expressionism began in Germany in the early years of the twentieth century.

expressive showing the emotions

Fauvism early twentieth-century style of art that uses extremely vivid colors, often in an unrealistic way. Leading Fauvist artists were Henri Matisse and André Derain.

flat color solid, unbroken, single color

folk art art practiced by craftworkers and country people, based on traditions that have lasted for hundreds of years

form shape of a figure or an object

graphic design design involving text, such as book and poster design

Impressionism late nineteenth-century style of art that aims to show the impression that a scene makes on the artist's senses. The Impressionists used bright colors and bold brushstrokes.

innovative original and creative

Japonism general name to describe the art and crafts of Japan. The name *Japonism* was born as a result of the craze for Japanese style that swept through Europe and the United States in the second half of the nineteenth century.

landscape painting painting of a view of natural scenery

mainstream the main, current, or most popular trend

media different materials or art forms that an artist can use, such as paint, sculpture, or pastels

mural large-scale painting on a wall

Nabis group of French artists founded by Sérusier in the late 1880s. The Nabis included Bonnard and Vuillard. They painted striking pictures influenced by Japanese art, and worked in various kinds of decorative and graphic arts.

Neo-Impressionism late nineteenth-century movement in French painting led by Seurat and Signac, who created paintings using pointillist techniques

Op Art style of art that began in the 1960s, in which artists experiment with optical effects. Op Art is short for optical art.

optical mixing process by which the brain of the viewer mixes colors together when they are placed side by side

optics the science of how we see things

palette choice of colors used in an artist's work or a board on which an artist mixes colors

pastel soft, chalklike crayon, used by artists

perspective technique used by artists to show the relationship between close and distant objects

philosopher someone who thinks deeply about difficult subjects, such as the meaning of life and art

pointillism technique in which paint is applied in dots of pure color. When viewed from a distance, the dots appear to merge together and the colors appear brighter and more intense.

primary colors colors—red, blue, and yellow—that cannot be made from a mixture of other colors

principles guidelines or rules for people to use

South Sea islanders people from the islands of the South Pacific

still life painting or drawing showing objects that are not alive

studio artist's workshop

stylized shown in a deliberately artistic way, using a definite style

subject figure or scene depicted by an artist

symbol something that represents or stands for something else

symbolism movement in art, music, and literature that began in France and Belgium in the late nineteenth century. Symbolist artists use images with a personal or religious meaning.

three-dimensional having three dimensions: width, height, and depth. When something is painted to look three-dimensional, it seems solid and not flat.

woodblock print block of wood that is cut or carved so that an image is left in relief. Colored ink is then applied to the raised image, and the image is pressed against paper to create a print.

Find Out More

Useful websites

General sites on Post-Impressionism, with examples of Post-Impressionist works

www.artcyclopedia.com
A large site describing different art styles including Post-Impressionism. Click on the links to find out information on different Post-Impressionist artists, with many examples of Post-Impressionist works from museums and public galleries.

www.artlex.com
An online art dictionary. Click on "Pon-Pq" in the left sidebar, then scroll down to "Post-Impressionism". This links to pages showing examples of works by individual artists. Click on "Ne-Nz" in the Home Page sidebar to find "Neo Impressionism" for information on Seurat and his followers.

www.metmuseum.org/toah/hd/poim/hd_poim.htm
An illustrated essay from the Metropolitan Museum, New York, on the major Post-Impressionists, with links to sites on individual artists.

Sites featuring individual artists or groups

www.artic.edu/aic/exhibitions/seurat/seurat_themes.html
A site describing the life and works of Seurat, including information on his color theory and the making of *La Grande Jatte*.

www.expo-cezanne.com
A virtual gallery of 300 works by Cézanne, searchable on theme, title, date, and technique. Also includes a biography of the artist.

www.expo-gauguin.net
A virtual gallery of 300 works by Gauguin, searchable on theme, title, date, and technique. Also includes a biography of the artist.

www.expo-vangogh.com
A virtual gallery of 300 paintings by Van Gogh, searchable on theme, title, date, and technique. Also includes a biography of the artist.

www.nga.gov/collection/gallery/gg82/gg82-main1.html
A website by the National Gallery of Art, Washington, D.C. Presents paintings by Gauguin in the museum's collection with helpful commentaries.

www.nga.gov/exhibitions/2006/cezanne/index.shtm
A website by the National Gallery of Art, Washington, D.C.

www.nga.gov/exhibitions/vgwel.shtm
A website by the National Gallery of Art, Washington, D.C. Presents a virtual tour of the museum's exhibition "Van Gogh's Van Goghs."

www.vangoghgallery.com
A large site on Vincent van Gogh. Includes collections of Van Gogh's paintings, drawings, and self-portraits. The site also contains sections on the artist's biography and extracts from his letters.

www.sdmart.org/lautrec
A website from the San Diego Museum of Art devoted to the poster art of Toulouse-Lautrec.

www.charleston.org.uk
A site devoted to Vanessa Bell's house at Charleston in England, decorated by members of the Bloomsbury Group of artists.

More books to read

Bolton, Linda. *Artists in Profile: Post-Impressionists*. Chicago: Heinemann Library, 2002.

Thomson, Belinda. *The Post-Impressionists*. New York: Phaidon Press, 1995.

O'Reilly, Wenda. *Van Gogh and Friends Art Book*. Palo Alto, Cal.: Birdcage Press, 2002.

Further research

Why not extend your studies, by searching the Internet or by looking in books? You could find out about some less well-known artists who worked in Post-Impressionist styles, or movements, styles, and groups closely related to Post-Impressionism.

Post-Impressionists working in France

Louis Anquetin, Emile Bernard, Pierre Bonnard, Henri-Edmond Cross, Maurice Denis, Camille Pissarro, Lucien Pissarro, Paul Ranson, Félix Vallotton, Édouard Vuillard

Post-Impressionists working outside France

Vanessa Bell, Roger Fry, Harold Gilman, Spencer Gore, Duncan Grant, Maurice Prendergast, Théo van Rysselberghe

Other art movements, styles, and groups

Art Nouveau
Symbolism
Japonism
Omega Workshops
Expressionism
Fauvism
Cubism

Disclaimer

All the Internet addresses (URLs) given in this book were valid at the time of going to press. However, owing to the dynamic nature of the Internet, some addresses may have changed or sites may have ceased to exist since publication. Although the author, packager, and publishers regret any inconvenience this may cause readers, no responsibility for any such change can be accepted by the author, packager, or publishers.

Index